"MAY YOU BE BLESSED
UPON YOUR JOURNEY
AND MAY YOU ALWAYS
REMEMBER WHO YOU ARE
AND BE EXACTLY THAT."

A Horse
Carries Me

Paula D. Fauth

Published by Elliot Rivers Publishing Co. 2016

Elliot Rivers Co. is a Wyoming State Incorporation.

PO Box 164, Cody, Wyoming 82414

Editing services provided by Leslie Forbes Heibel.

For information address Elliot Rivers Co.,

P.O. Box 164, Cody, Wyoming 82414

ISBN - 13: 978-1523679966

ISBN - 10: 1523679964

Printed in the U.S.A.

A HORSE CARRIES ME *is dedicated to my parents, Linda and Willis. They gave me Elliot Rivers, a chestnut quarter horse who became the inspiration horse that destined me to a unique and purposeful life. Their love and support has been steadfast all the days of my life. They are the kindest and most generous people I know. If I can be a fraction of the person they are, then I will have made the world a better place, as have they.*

- My love forever to you both

CONTENTS

DEAR FRIENDS

*I have made a journey
through these pages based
on moments inspired by
nature and horses.*

I BEGAN THESE PAGES FOR

myself so that I would not forget. I would not forget who I truly am, deep inside the depths of my being. So that I would not forget who others are and respect their story and journey; so that I would remember that everything is energy, nothing is ever as it seems, and that I am a player within this one little place in time and that place and time is infinite. Too often, I live as if I am merely stating my lines, standing on stage for the first time, a wild-eyed seven year old, with butterflies twirling inside. Too often, the days of my life have been full of forgetting and filled with merely responding or acting out what is expected. Therefore, I have made a journey through these pages based on moments inspired by nature and horses. My inspiration early in life was my horse, Elliot Rivers. I rode on his back, devoted hours tending to his daily care, and ripened to the mystery of this living and my role within it. The more time I spent in nature, the more my mind and senses calmed and I discovered a strong, unshakable presence deep inside .

It was during the transition time of going from my own two feet to the rhythmic movement of my four-legged friend that gave me visions into the future and the meaning of life. This time showed me who I was to be and what I was to do with my life. It instructed me on life lessons that I wish I could remember each and every day. However, I discovered that due to the constant outside chaos of trying to live within a system that is drumming its demands upon us, I often forget what I know at my core. I am older now and have lived a life that has brought much adventure, deep love, and life lessons that have spawned a thirst for wisdom and knowing, but I have shyly skirted around what I know I was meant to be and do in my role for this life. Truthfully, I still feel as if I'm on stage, seven years old, giggling nervously because I have forgotten my lines and don't know what to do next. Thus, I write to remember, to prompt, to encourage, to rejuvenate, and to act. It is my wish that these "remembrances" will somehow do the exact same for you.

May you be blessed upon your journey and may you always REMEMBER who you are and be exactly that.

Remember that everything is energy, nothing is ever as it seems, and that you are a player within this one little place in time, and that place and time is infinite.

You are infinite.

A HORSE CARRIES ME

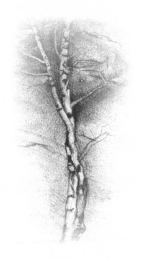

*..another moment in
true synchronicity...*

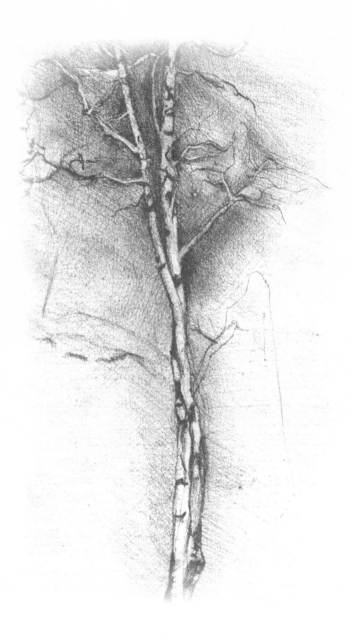

A HORSE CARRIES ME

On with footsteps you and I go,
our tracks land soft in the leaf covered grove.
You with four and I with two,
you feel confident as well as I do.

We both know the time is right,
from six steps to four in the soft light.
Upon your back you gently carry me,
gladly avoiding any branches there may be.

Cautious of your precious load,
a friend you carry and with love I glow.
My body slips into your walking rhythm,
as your hoof beats tell me that I've been given.

Another moment in true synchronicity,
and I'm happy to let it be.
When nature's close and letting me see,
more of her than if it was just me.

THE TRAIL

*..there's a beautiful
place waiting for you..*

THERE WAS A BLISSFUL PATH

I traveled as a youth. It wandered through a leaf covered grove of aspens that led to a pond and a small meadow. Here, I would sit and look through the cathedral of branches and leaves as they danced against the blue sky above. I had a good friend, Elliot Rivers, who took me to this place. He had four legs, I had two, and he gently accepted me as his cargo. We became great companions, communicating with each other in quiet understanding.

Elliot was a plain looking chestnut quarter horse, but he had a presence about him that was noticeable and different than the other horses in the pasture. It was a calming factor mixed with a sense of wisdom and nobility. There was a sweet gentleness that seemed to make everything and everyone around him relax. In other horses, the herd mentality dominated their every move. With Elliot, there was a deep sense of knowing, like he had traveled through the ages and knew something unspoken and sacred.

Riding Elliot transported me from the sidelines of nature's edge. I now floated through it, fitted into a worn out saddle atop this great steed, galloping along the serpentine terrain, free as the water flowed. Riding Elliot was discovery and I found the time spent with him a natural meditation where I could experience nature up close. The foxes, birds, racoons, and deer were not afraid of Elliot and as I was part of him, they were no longer cautious of me, allowing me a peek into their private and wild world.

It was in this wonder that I could go deep into myself and receive instant answers for any question asked. There was a connection to something larger than myself, at work through myself. Our rides became spiritual journeys and discussions of life, hope, love, and the great abundance of spirit that I felt in the landscape. It was where I learned about the part of life not taught within the compounds of my bricked up school or lined up desk.

Elliot was my bliss and my view of life became cast through the filters of the lessons and joy I gleamed from him. I could trust the lessons that nature and him taught, whereas my human teachers were sometimes unintentionally tripped-up by their untrained ego's desire to be manipulative, selfish, and concerned with nothing other than a physical, outward life. Sadly, it seems that anything that brings great bliss, stays for only an instant, and the workings of this physical dimension produce the "bliss-ters" which develop from those things that rub at us, causing a discomfort that we must eventually deal with and heal.

Unfortunately, the majority of our days on the earth seem spent not following our bliss or staying in situations that don't make us happy. These are the desolate situations that suck the very life force out of us. They can be a physical place, person, job, or situation, which function as a distraction, taking our energy and leaving us feeling exhausted, thirsty, and worn out.

Reminding ourselves of moments, when we experienced pure joy and happiness, helps us to return to that which once made us happy and "blissful". These memories can motivate us towards a better place. Trusting the feeling of joy, we discover things will appear to help us with our burdens and our needs are fulfilled as we trust the path. Sometimes your happiness resides in a place you may not expect to find it. However, once you're on your true life path and following your bliss, you'll discover there's a beautiful place waiting for you. This place is abundant and fits you perfectly, whatever that may be, and you find it easily because it's been there all along.

It's a constant journey, and one we must take daily, to finding this pattern of feeling complete and happy. We must have blind courage to put ourselves in the precarious and unknown position of taking and trusting the path that feels right to us.

It has been many years since I picked my way

along that path into the aspen grove riding atop Elliot. I believe that engrained deep within the Book of Life are the horses' footprints and essence. In the chapter on my soul there's mention of a great horse named Elliot Rivers, who was destined to be grazing in a field, waiting for me to saddle him up, so we could ride the path that was there waiting for us all along.

Trust your feelings of joy
and follow them.
Things will appear that
help you with your burdens
and your needs
will be fulfilled
as you trust the path.

3

WISDOM WITHOUT WORDS

..I imagined he was some kind of a messenger..

ALL I DO IS WAIT FOR WORDS.

I wait for them to appear in my thoughts so I can string them into sentences. I wait for them to come out of my being so I can express to those around me what I am thinking, feeling, or needing. I wait on them from those I love, wishing I would hear what I so desperately need to: That I am loved, I am worthy, I am desired and needed.

In Genesis, God spoke and everything was created. It is the word we use to navigate our way through life and even at a whisper its power is monumental, taking us to great heights of happiness or deep depths of despair. The words are constantly being breathed out all around us, creating a pattern to everything we do and feel.

There are also the words inside. That constant voice that chatters away inside our heads. Is that our own voice? If so, why is it mostly destructive? This voice often focuses on fear and insecurities. There are constant reminders from these internal words that I am not good enough, or pretty enough, successful enough, loved enough; nothing is ever enough when it comes to this voice and its words. I have to work at directing my internal words to tell me loving things and remind me that I am a beautiful being full of light and joy, worthy of love and all the good things I am given.

When we are feeling chaotic or out of control with life, we use more words. I complain more, I talk constantly to my friends, trying to get the words to solve my problem. I use words to mask my true intentions or cover up my mistakes. They are my tool of choice when I desire to deceive. I foolishly use them in hurtful ways, usually with those I love the most. Then, I try more words to express my apologies and soon, the person I love the most discovers that my words may not be trusted.

Life for a person is all about words. Words are a grand riddle and the only time they can really be trusted is when you become silent, stop the chattering madness and enter that space where the true words can come through. When there are no words, just a smile, a lock of the eyes, a touch of a hand, or a soft kiss, everything "said" is more powerful than any words could ever be.

To solve our problems, share our intended communications, and keep our intentions pure, we must first abandon the words.

I'm reminded of the teachings of an old friend of mine. As a youth, I walked a half mile from where the bus dropped me off to my house. I cut across a field and took a path that led through the aspen grove. There was a downed log where I liked to sit, watch, and listen. One day I sat there silently for some time and when I looked up, to my delight, an owl was sitting in the branches directly above me. His gray spotted feathers camouflaged him within the white and black spotted aspens so much so, I didn't know he had been there watching me the entire time. Once I noticed him and our eyes made contact he flew away. I imagined he was some kind of a messenger.

On repeat visits to this part of the grove I hoped to encounter the owl. However, I discovered that if I walked into the grove and looked around, I could not find him. So, I would sit on the log, close my eyes, and get very quiet in my mind. Once I achieved complete silence and a feeling that I was a part of the natural environment - like the dirt, leaves, and trees - I'd look into the branches. To my total amazement, the owl would be directly above me, having been sitting there the entire time. We played this game often and each time it was the same; I couldn't see him until I was truly present and had slowed everything down inside myself so that a deep quietness resided. Through that presence I became a part of my surroundings.

As I grew in life, I found that when I find this quietness inside, things become clear, solutions to problems appear, and talk that restlessly floats around in my mind, is drowned by the soft rustle of nature's deepest teaching - presence. If we strive to be truly present in each and every moment, we experience a peace inside and a sense of wisdom and true knowing. The wisdom is present without the words.

This presence and silence is the key to everything in life and nature teaches us well about its power. It's the key to communicating with others in a loving and effective way. If we're clear with our thoughts and communication, we'll enjoy a harmonious relationship. Trust the silence and allow it to be present within your life and speak your words from it.

Today, we focus on constant "talk" and constant "noise". It is there to distract us and help us forget our power and beauty. Blending ourselves with things like cell phones is a noisy and disruptive business that doesn't promote our strengths as a human, but hinders us in ways we haven't even discovered yet.

The mind's tendancy is to think only of survival, the day's events, and gossip. When we tap into a deeper level of thought, which is activated by the miracles of life, the gazing at stars, the rhythms of nature, then we call forth a presence of reverence inside and we know that this is what we seek.

Our daily lives may require that we spend our time in the *words* of schools, offices, and city streets where we partake in the constant stream of strenuous life lessons, and the silence is broken, constantly broken. Only in the quiet times can we find wisdom that lingers under the surface within us and is beyond all words. In this silence lives the omnipotent wisdom which is circulating and available to us at all times.

Trust the silence.
Allow it to be present within.
Speak your words from it.

4

ENHANCING THE RELATIONSHIP

..life is ONLY about relationships..

MANY YEARS AGO, I WROTE this sentence: "When you start enhancing one relationship it opens up an entire universe of awareness and many things will benefit." Only now do I truly grasp how big of a statement this really is because I have come to know that life is ONLY about relationships. Our food, families, dirt, work, everything is all about how we are relating to it and it to us. Food grown in soil that is nourished with rich nutrients and lovingly cultivated gives us more vitamins and a healthier life. It's this way with absolutely everything upon the earth. Everything is relations. There's nothing any of us do void of a relationship.

Early on in life I settled upon the horse as the one thing I listened to more than anything else. A horse operates solely through relating. When your hand is raised around a horse, it instantly gives you feedback as to what type of relationship you are creating. They know if your hand is raised in love or aggression and they act accordingly. The horse is unique in the way it can provide real-time feedback about ourselves and if we are creating a positive relationship or a negative one.

Oliver was the horse who taught me about the intricacies of relationships. He was a horse accustomed to the game of manipulation and aggression that human beings play. Before he came to my pasture, Oliver had been through it all. He'd been a show horse, a race horse, a hunter/jumper, a reining horse, and a trail horse. As I did ordinary daily chores in his pasture, I saw scars exposed from things he'd endured.

The first time I used a pitchfork to clean his paddock he ran tight along the fence trying to escape. The same was true if I picked up a stick in his vicinity, he bolted.

Realizing he'd obviously been hit or threatened

by these types of objects, I started to tell him, "No one is ever going to hurt you again, Oliver." I repeated this phrase until my words and their intention sunk into the very marrow of his bones and I matched the words with my actions of gentleness. It took a good amount of time for Oliver to forget the memories of a stick, pitchfork, shovel or anything that looked like it might be used with force upon his body.

As we spent our days together and grew trust in each other, I eventually could pick up a stick or the pitchfork and run it gently atop his back or swing it around him and he would merely nap. He came to trust me and knew that I wasn't going to hurt him. We healed that old relationship memory.

By working with Oliver I realized that I needed to heal from my own past hurts caused by a harmful word or hand. I saw how staying stuck in old hurts and toxic relationship patterns makes us lose joyous parts of our present lives. Plus, it can cause interference with truly good relationships in our life because we're allowing old memories of hurt and harm to bitter us and hold us back from accepting love.

With a horse, what you see is what you get. With a human, there are masks worn and we can be extremely talented at tricking each other into the belief that we are true.

Navigating the manipulations, doing and behaving in ways we think we're supposed to, throws us into loss of our true selves. We get into relationships and suffer profound hurt over and over again, whereas we should be acting like Oliver; when the instrument used to hurt us is in view, we should run. We shouldn't stick around to take a "beating", and by doing this we make those around us stop practicing hurtful behavior and prove to us they won't do it again, ever. It's really that simple. However, we sometimes choose to complicate everything with excuses like, "We can't leave because we don't have the money," or "We can't leave because what would people think of us," and so on. The brain churns out reasons why we must stay in a life of harm.

Sometimes I wonder if we spend our entire lives navigating our way around the manipulation of others, doing what they want us to do and trying to be what seems acceptable to them. There's always someone trying to control what we're doing, putting rules up so that we have to follow them, tricking us into believing something that doesn't serve our greater good. If we stopped relating to each other in these ways, the effects would be tremendous.

In the lesson of Oliver, it is clear that the only thing that busts through these old memories of hurt and harm is constant love and an intention that is pure, true, and built on harmony. We owe it to each other to help heal these wounds that seep from our souls. With Oliver, I saw first hand how from the internal intentions of a loving heart the outward actions flow and by practicing this, you will see the results all around you through harmony in your relations.

And when I'm feeling this love and purity of heart, I venture into the pasture where there's a beautiful horse named Oliver running to see me, because together we've learned that once both of us present ourselves as healed and complete beings, we enjoy a life of harmony and friendship. From this one simple friendship love grows and we feel happy as we venture into our day, passing that on into every relationship we have.

*Others are concerned for me and wish me
well upon this earth. They wish me to be
successful within this system of work, family,
money, accumulation of things; all the things
that appear to bring a life of happiness.*

*I, however, wish to be well and successful
in my spiritual path first, as I know this will
make all my earthly days well -
no matter what.*

5

WALKING RHYTHM

*..we have to
keep moving..*

M OVEMENT IS THE KEY TO

our temporal body's maintenance while we live upon this earth. The movement of breath and body keep the heart pumping and the veins cleaned out of debris. This in turn keeps all the good things circulating within, delivering the nourishment to the cells and maintaining the body's functions. The earth reflects this in everything; the waters path stays clean when flowing quickly and steadily, creating a fresh supply for those depending upon it. The oceans rock back and forth in constant movement and rhythms. Even the horse utilizes movement with the bottom of their foot acting as their heart's circulatory pump. Movement is the modus operandi of everything upon the earth.

There is a way to move and a way not to move. Moving in flowing motions while enjoying the movement is relaxing to the body, soul, and spirit. Moving in fear causes collapsing of airflow, tightening of muscles, and strain upon the heart. We all know the difference because we experience it daily.

A horse is a great teacher of fluid movement because you can't be rigid and it's best to not be fearful when you ride a horse.

One night I wanted to go for a ride on Elliot. It was early fall and this was my favorite time of the year. On this particular evening, I saddled Elliot and we rode down a small gravel road. The dusk turned into night and it was just him and me under the stars. I asked Elliot to go into a canter and we loped along the edge of the road. I couldn't see very well but knew he could, so I completely trusted him to stick to the road and keep us safe. In a split second, there was a rustle in the brush next to the road and Elliot made a giant leap away from it. My body was planning on staying in a straight, forward position. As he jumped to the left, I wasn't ready for it and wasn't quick enough to adapt. I went flying off of him and hit the dirt right on my shoulder blade and proceeded to roll a few times in the dirt and weeds.

Elliot stopped as soon as I fell off and stayed with me. I didn't waste time getting back in the saddle and riding off the dirt, as I'd learned early on from my riding instructor; if one falls off a horse, they must get right back on and ride it out. I kept Elliot in a walk back home as I was a little shaken from the fall. This was a night I would always remember - the first time I was thrown off a horse. I was amazed by the feeling of the fall and the rolling sensation more than anything and kept reliving the event in my mind. I felt blessed that the outcome of my night didn't include a broken bone or any head damage.

When we are in our youth, we don't think about things and we ride off in the night, feeling confident and free. As we have more experiences throughout life and we see the possibilities of what "could" happen, it can cause us to compartmentalize our lives and become paralyzed by the fear of what can go wrong. When this happens, movement stops. We don't keep moving, taking chances and making progress upon our life path. Once fear takes over, muscles become stiff and rigid, and we start bracing ourselves for impact. We expect something to harm us and we live with that threat inside, allowing fear to permeate the mind and hold us back. Whenever we try to see through the distances, wondering what's going to happen next, fear has set its nasty trap and we are caught.

We must remember to keep moving and to keep getting back on the horse. Movement starts within us by moving ourselves with confidence, letting go of the possible outcomes that play over in our mind, staying relaxed, and ready for anything that comes our way.

Keep walking, though there's no place to get to.
Don't try to see through the distances.
That's not for human beings. Move within.
But don't move the way fear makes you move.

- RUMI -

6

SLIPPING OFF THE CLIFF

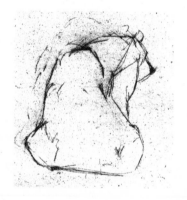

..obstacles along the trail..

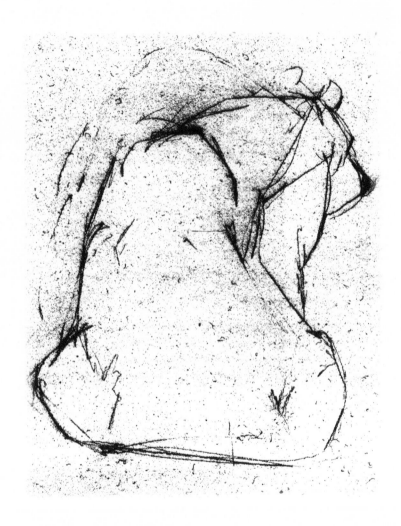

IT DOESN'T MATTER HOW

wonderful our lives are, if we are happy or rich, there will always be scratches, bruises, sometimes broken bones or heartache that snatch our joy. These are obstacles along the trail and we must stay alert and out of their way the best we can. This requires us to be hyper-alert, ducking to avoid things that can harm us, and learning how to use a powerful tool - the word "NO" said with intention.

In nature, there's no questioning or accommodating. The natural world operates by being exactly what it is; in a black and white, yes and no type format. A mama grizzly bear won't allow you around her cubs. She protects them at all costs, it's just who she is. Stay out of her territory and you'll be okay. Cross her path and you may be in serious danger. It's not personal. It's just the nature of a mama grizzly bear.

Could we actually say "NO" to something that didn't fit us or was threatening us? Could we be honest and only do those things that are in alignment with our true nature?

In working with a horse they have the desire to be a willing partner because they believe that cooperation is what will enable their survival. This is a trait true to their nature. A dog is our best friend because it lives best in a pack scenario where the pack is a family, caring for one another, enjoying playful games, teaming up in food gathering, and so it works that we are companions with these animals. Of course we can lend human qualities to all animals through training them, but even the best trained creature keeps the undercurrent of what they are based on their natural instincts.

Too often we accept life as presented to us by others, or we want to be part of the group, so we go along with something that doesn't quite feel right. By doing this over and over again, we dampen that protective feature that burns within our guts and sends out the signal when something isn't in our best interests. We do this innocently without knowing it. We agree to things because we feel insecure in allowing our true feelings to be exposed and we stay silent and do things that are out of our level of honor or comfort.

We accommodate. We question our self worth, our internal knowing and think others know best. We accommodate their ideas, thoughts, and feelings, even when we know something may not be right. We don't speak up because we're unsure how they'd take our standing up to them or questioning them, so we reside to keep quiet and acquiesce.

When we go against our internal "NO" and we accommodate something or allow our awareness to be distracted, it's usually us or something we love that gets hurt. I've had many experiences like this in real life, but sometimes I will have a dream that teaches me about a concept or life lesson that I am to learn or become aware of.

In one particular dream, Elliot and I were walking down a small road in the mountains. The road was full of steep curves and there was a large drop off on one side. There was no halter on Elliot or a lead rope connecting us; we were just walking in harmony. It was just the two of us and I was happy.

Soon, four people came walking up the road. They were people I knew and they said, "Can we come with you?" A deep sense inside instantly said "NO", but I didn't want to make them feel bad, so I said, "Yes you can."

The six of us proceeded down the steep mountain road and the four people talked a lot and were distracting to both Elliot and I. All of us were walking side by side but the road was too narrow to handle that. Elliot got too close to the edge, lost his footing and slipped off the road. He started to roll and tumble down the cliff. I watched in horror as I knew he was breaking every bone in his body and that he was probably going to die. I was in a panic and lost my own footing and started to fall down the cliff as well. He hit the bottom first and then me. We both laid there for a moment in silence. Elliot was able to get up and didn't appear injured. I got up and and I was okay, too. By this time, the four people had caught up to us and were standing there staring at us, saying nothing, nor helping. Without a doubt, I put my hand up and in a strong voice told them "NO, you can't come with us," and we moved forward on the path.

A sacred teaching dream like this provides a fascinating explanation for so many concepts. It shows how easy it is to feel a "NO" but say "YES" and give in to something that doesn't feel right. Their constant talking was such a distraction that it literally forced Elliot and I off the path and we ended up being the ones who tumbled down the cliff, not them, nor did they help us in any way.

Even simple accommodations can create results that may greatly influence a project you are working on, a friendship, or your health. Accommodating happens anytime we're not speaking openly about something that truly is interfering with our true natures, concentration, or honor - it interferes with our life path. It happens when we allow another person to control and influence us, even though we are aware inside that we should say "NO" to them. We allow accommodations because we don't want to hurt someone's feelings or we lack enough confidence in ourselves to speak our truth. It's okay for us to protect ourselves from things or people that will take selfishly, distract us, and possibly hurt us.

Our true natures are to give freely and openly in life. And true giving results in a healthy and mutual giving and a genuine caring for each other with no strings attached.

If we put as much effort into accommodating our own natures as we do in accommodating others, we'd be much easier on ourselves. There's power in understanding ourselves and choosing that which best fits us and makes us stay harmonious to both our inner and outer lives. What if we not only did this for ourselves, but we supported each other in doing so, as well? Imagine the possibilities.

Wherever a horse is,
so is inspiration.
Wherever a horse is,
so is a dream.

7

GIVEN

..be the first to give a second chance..

THERE'S ONE THING IN LIFE

we can rest assured in: We are given breath which sustains us as we learn and grow in this earthly playground and eventually, we are given over to our last one. In between these breaths is where we are given the time to do and redo, mix and remix, assure and be reassured, be joyful and rejoice.

Life gives us a lot of opportunity to create something wonderful and hopefully this is the case, but when things don't go as planned, life gives us something even more important, a second chance.

It was Oliver who taught me about second chances, both giving and receiving them. When Elliot passed on,

Oliver came along. It's important for me to interject that my horse training abilities are zero. I am enamoured with the horse but not necessarily a skilled horseperson or a master of horsemanship. I was lucky because Elliot was a great horse and well-trained long before he came into my life. Oliver, however, presented an entirely new way of thinking. Here was a well-trained show horse, broken and wrecked; this horse needed to be "untrained" of everything he knew and in an odd way, I was the perfect person to accomplish this.

Oliver wasn't on track to live a long life. He was on his way to slaughter when his second chance came. I'm not sure Oliver really wanted this second chance to be kept alive. He was lame in two legs, had a bacterial infection on all four legs from standing in mud, had a bad hip, ring bone in one leg and was very thin. Plus, when the vet pulled his shoes, he found two severe abscesses caused from the nails for his shoes being pounded into his hoof cavity. The vet advised me to consider putting this gift horse down, but there was an unspoken agreement between Oliver and myself. The vet didn't know that I had met this horse three years prior and had tried to adopt him then, but it hadn't worked out. Then one day, out of the blue, the phone rang and Oli was delivered the next morning.

Oli was broken in every way - spirit, body, and heart - and this majestic, beautiful creature was a wretched beast of anger, pain, and distrust. With so many physical problems, Oliver required my constant attention. I had to soak his feet twice a day in epsom salts, boot up two feet, which is a chore in itself, give him a scrubbing on all four legs with a special anti-bacterial soap and feed him small, frequent batches of hay and grain so that he could put on weight slowly and steadily.

I was not enjoying having to be tied down by this horse because I had recently gone through a divorce and the death of Elliot. I was sad in my heart. I wanted to run away and disappear into the forest or out on the ocean on a sailing ship. Instead, I was stuck caring for this horse and the odd part was that something inside of me was superiorly devoted to him. Oliver was my second chance, too. When I spent time with him, it gave me a chance to care about something other than my own problems. He was like a lighthouse to the neighborhood, drawing all sorts of new people to his pasture to inquire about him and learn his story.

It wasn't easy to care for him either, Oliver would fight me on everything. He had trigger zones on his body that the gentlest of touch would cause him to snap and bite. Most people would have disciplined a horse for doing this, but I reacted like I would if anyone bit me, I screamed out in pain and jumped back, and sometimes I ran away from him. Instead of pressing the issue, I knew that I needed to give this horse space.

A few months passed. The abscesses were healed and my friend, Sarah, who was a Naturopathic doctor, gave me a salve mixture that healed Oli's bacterial infection in lightning quick fashion. He had also gained a nice amount of weight and his ribs were no longer in view or hip bones protruding out.

Oliver and I became friends in small advances. I started to earn his trust slowly. Over time he relaxed and came to know me as a helper and as someone he could trust.

Oli had been a great show horse, but never just a horse. He was tense and anxious when halters and ropes were brought out. I knew it was time to let him be a horse.

My friend and neighbor, Darlene, owned fifty acres. She and her husband, Don, would stop to see Oli everyday on their way to town. It wasn't long after Oli came to me that Darlene lost Don, her husband of many years. She shared with me how much Don enjoyed seeing Oliver and he referred to him as "his horse". Darlene invited Oli to come live at her farm and I quickly accepted the opportunity.

I knew this was going to be Oliver's chance to be a horse. He could stretch his legs and graze in big, grassy pastures, which would help his ringbone situation as well as his hip. This horse needed to move.

The day I walked him the short distance down the road to her place and into the big, beautiful pasture, I told Oliver that he was going to be free and I took off the halter and let him go.

I rarely haltered Oliver after I set him free and what took place was profound in our relationship. I visited him daily to check on his well-being and every day he grew fatter and healthier and started to walk with less of a limp in the ringbone leg. I learned about a trimming method used to help with ringbone and I started to practice it on him. Soon, he started to run again and continued to do so for the rest of his life.

Oli and I started a grand friendship. I would sit on a large boulder in his pasture and he would stand with his head hanging directly above mine and take a nap, eventually his mouth would come to rest on the top of my head. Oliver and I enjoyed the next eleven years together and he became the gentlest horse I'd ever had.

Oli was given a second chance to be a horse and he did so gloriously.

When we're at a state in our life where we've failed or "wrecked", there's usually a moment when someone shows up to help or some "miracle" happens that will give us a second chance. Don't think about it, just take it. Too often we think we aren't deserving or worthy of a second chance, but we are. When life gives us any opportunity to make ourselves better or heals us in some way, it's worth accepting. In the same way, second chances are worth giving. Be the first to give a second chance to someone. Apologize first, love them first, give to them first, help them first, and rejoice in the fact that you can give someone or something such a precious gift.

Inevitably, there's a day when we won't be given a second chance, it will be the finale of our life. As for me, I'm convinced that when this body of mine has had enough, and I'm given into my last breath, there will be a second chance in the spirit. I imagine I will be at one of my favorite places; the base of the Big Horn Mountains, walking on one of the long, grassy plateaus that stretches out into the prairie. I will see Elliot and Oliver running towards me in the distance along with my friends and family who will greet me in these grasslands of Heaven and welcome me home.

When life gives you an opportunity to make
yourself better or heals you in some way,
it's worth accepting.

8

RECONCILE

*..the biggest task we
have as a person
upon the earth...*

RELATIONSHIPS REQUIRE

reconciliation repeatedly. To reconcile is to restore that which was once in harmony back to harmony. Personally, I reconcile with something or someone on a daily basis. It seems easier to slip out of harmony in relationships than to maintain it. My first tendency is to be stubborn like a bull, fast to distrust, and quick to put my horns down ready for a fight. These are defensive behaviors that eventually become habits and characteristics. Unfortunately, these behaviors become our first choice, forgiveness and compassion, the second.

Before we can have harmony outside ourselves, we must first reconcile and regain harmonious relations within and stop the source of the fight. True love, compassion, and forgiveness can only be given to others when we have it for ourselves. I will boldly say that this could be the biggest task we have as a person upon this earth - the task of reconciling ourselves.

Self-reconciliation starts with knowing who you are as a human being. It's not self-absorbed knowing. It's about knowing what is the core of you as a soul, spirit, body, and mind. It's about knowing and loving the person that fits into this grandly orchestrated universe. It's about knowing what your specific role is and sharing that. You can only find out what your role is by knowing who you truly are. When we don't know why we exist and why we are here it creates a severe disruption in our harmony inside. We don't feel valuable nor do we see why any of our actions are worthwhile. We feel as if we don't matter.

Joy helps jog the memory of who you are and is one of the first steps to restoring harmony within. I remember a friend telling me, "When you feel bad, stop and go back to the last time you felt good and start over from there." It was simple advice but powerful. A horse or a walk in nature is a great tool for resetting joy and stopping the fight inside. Whatever it is that brings you joy, once you put it at the forefront of your life, you'll discover that in the greater and grander scheme of things, a lot of what we allow to disturb us isn't really that important.

As you open to the great joy and love of who you are remember to protect yourself from the scar talk of others. Everyone has had both good and bad experiences in life but their story will in no way be your story. Your story is completely unique. Sharing information about ourselves and our deepest thoughts and feelings can easily be shot down with words from another person. Sometimes we can be so influenced by others that we actually follow the path they choose for us and find ourselves feeling empty and consumed with a bitter fight inside. Start from the strong voice of joy, keep it alive by nourishing and protecting it, and live your life from there.

Another important task in getting back to harmony

within ourselves is in reconciling with expectations. Expectations can be the dagger in the heart that kills all progress and relationships. None of us know how the day's journey will go. We all desire love, success, and happiness, but they greet each of us differently. Watch out for starched expectations; they can leave you stranded and without anything because you held too tightly to the way you thought things were supposed to be rather than letting the way expose itself, as does a flower in the spring time.

Working with a horse teaches you to leave expectations at the gate. A horse expects you to be a leader and they operate from your clear intentions and directions, however, the way you achieve your goals with them may be completely different than you expected. A simple task with my Belgian draft horse, Arthur, is often full of surprises. Arthur was a dude ranch horse that had to be sold because he spooked easily on the trail and put people in danger. This is an issue I constantly work with Arthur on. One summer evening I thought I would treat Arthur to a bath and splash in the river, which he loves. I haltered him and we proceeded to walk through a sizable grassy pasture towards the river. A little way down the trail, Arthur planted his feet in a dead stop, snorting and sniffing. I saw the cause for his distress; a raccoon was ahead of us on the trail. So we simply changed our route. We were almost halfway to the river when we passed by some brush and scared a deer. The deer's sudden leaps and running sent Arthur into a leap back, a quick turn, and then a run back to the corral where we had started. I walked back after him and took a minute to calm him down before we continued on our expedition to the river. This time, with the deer gone, the raccoon most likely hidden away in a log, our path was clear and easy and we arrived at our destination.

Arthur and I accomplished our simple mission, however, it took a few twists and turns that were unexpected. Thus is the daily journey of life. We will usually arrive exactly where we are supposed to be, it just may not always be like we expect. If we expect the unexpected as we go through life, we can be more harmonious with both others and ourselves. If things don't go as planned, give up the urge to fight it and look for a different way to get to the same destiny.

One of the most important pieces in reconciling with ourselves is through being compassionate with ourselves. It's natural for us to be aware of the suffering of another being and act on the desire to help or relieve that suffering in any way we possibly can. However, we are not taught that the first act of compassion we must have begins with ourselves. We must do whatever it takes to heal and relieve our own suffering, first. When you are suffering inside and aren't able to restore a sense of peace within, you emanate this into all your actions and words and pass this on to others.

Compassion with ourselves stems first from self love and that happens when we take time to understand who we are, love who we are, and explore how we're going to share ourselves with the world.

It probably will take most of us a lifetime to come to love our beings completely and to be compassionate with ourselves, but in doing so, we will be blessed with one of the best relationships we could ever have, the one with ourselves.

"Compassionate with yourself,
you reconcile all beings."
- LAO TZU -

Made in the USA
Monee, IL
22 January 2022

89525929R00052